Audubon's Birds

Author: John James Audubon

Page 4:
Bald Eagle, Haliaeetus leucocephalus
Plate 11, Falconine Birds

Layout:
Baseline Co Ltd
Fiditourist, 3rd Floor
127- 129a Nguyen Hue Boulevard
District 1, Ho Chi Minh City
Vietnam

Published in 2006 by Grange Books
an imprint of Grange Books Plc
The Grange Kingsnorth Industrial Estate
Hoo, nr Rochester, Kent ME3 9ND
www.grangebooks.co.uk

ISBN 10 : 1-84013-942-0
ISBN 13 : 978-1-84013-942-6

Printed in China

Foreword

"I am well-received everywhere, my works praised and admired, and my poor heart is at last relieved from the great anxiety that has for so many years agitated it, for I now know that I have not worked in vain."

— John James Audubon, 1826

Biography

1785: John James Audubon is born on the island of Santo Domingo (now Haiti) on 26 April, son of a French sea captain and plantation owner, and his mistress.

1789: Arrives in France where he spends his childhood raised by his stepmother, Mrs Audubon. There, he takes a lively interest in birds, nature and drawing.

1803: Settles in America to escape conscription into the Emperor Napoleon's army.

1805: Returns to France.

1806: Goes back to America to escape the emperor's army again.

1808: Marries Lucy Bakewell.

1809: Birth of his son Victor Gifford, first of his two boys (the second named John Woodhouse).

1810: Receives a visit from Alexander Wilson, one of the first ornithologist painters of America. He realises his drawings are better than Wilson's so he decides to produce a work on all American Birds. Settles with his family in Henderson, Kentucky.

1820: Moves to Cincinnati and follows the Mississippi towards the south to discover the birds of Louisiana (which meant at that time a quarter of the American continent). There he meets the last free Indians.

John J. Audubon

1826:   He sails to Europe to raise money for the printing of his *Birds of America* and presents his work to the English botanists.

1826:   First plate printed.

1828:   Presentation of his work to the French botanists, meets Pierre Redouté.

1829:   Goes back to America to fulfil his study of birds.

1831-1839: Publication of his *Ornithological Biographies* in five volumes.

1832:   Expedition in the Carolinas anc in Florida to observe tropical birds.

1833:   Expedition to Labrador, Canada, on the settlements of arctic nesting.

1837:   Expedition in Texas.

1834:   Starts his exploration of West America.

1838:   His 435th and last plate is printed on 20 June.

1843:   Last expedition of Audubon to Yellowstone River.

1845-1848: Publication of the *Viviparous Quadrupeds of North America*.

1851:   John James Audubon dies on 27 January.

1886:   Founding of the National Audubon Society.

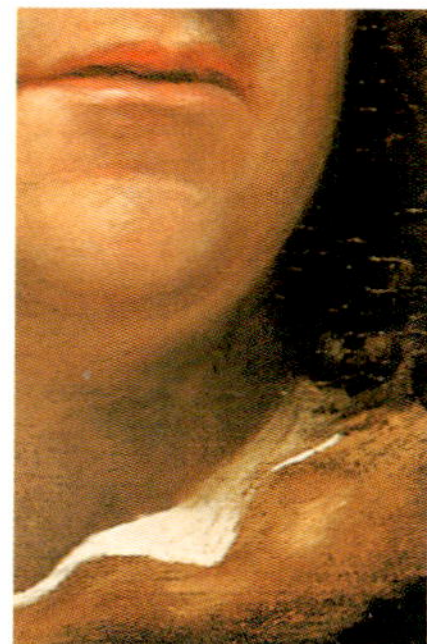

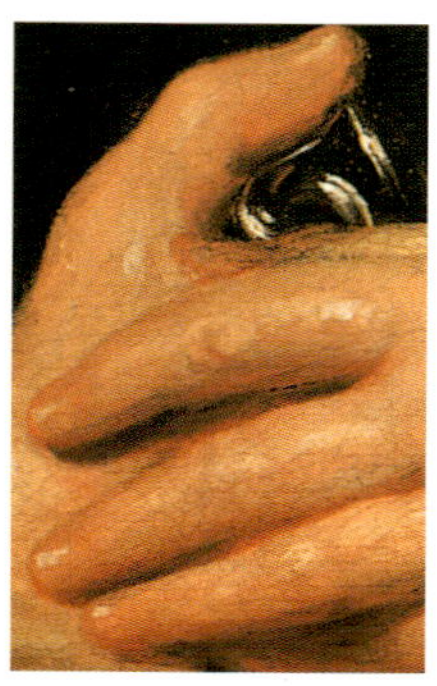

Preface

"Audubon could have been anything: a great philosopher, a great orator, a great poet, a great statesman, a Jean-Jacques Rousseau, a Montesquieu, a Chateaubriand. However, he was unable to be other than a naturalist, painter, and American ornithologist, a Buffon of the Northern States, but a Buffon of genius, spending his life in virgin forests and writing with the enthusiasm of solitude a few pages of the great animal epic of creation." (Lamartine, *Cours familier de littérature*, Paris, 1865).

Portrait of John James Audubon

John Syme, 1826
The White House Collection, Washington D.C.

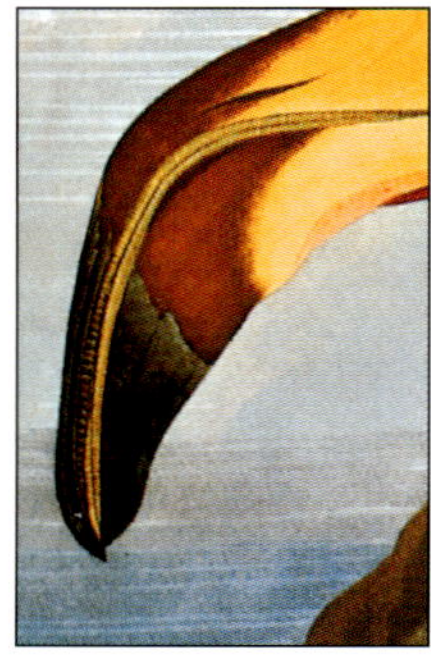

When John James Audubon decided after his meeting with Alexander Wilson in 1810 to paint and describe all the birds of North America, surely he never imagined that it would entail a lifetime of travels, scientific as well as artistic discoveries, and a pursuit of quality to the final proof of the published prints. That is the personality of this French American ornithologist, unique in his field, who succeeded in describing and illustrating all birds of the North American continent, there where his predecessors were confined to the former French and British colonies to the explored territories.

Greater Flamingo

Phoenicopterus ruber
Plate 431
Ducks

Yet, his legacy does not stop there. The originality of his illustrations marks a turning point in the history of representing nature. Audubon's depictions are life size, thus requiring him to multiply the number of birds appearing on the same plate, or bend the necks of others as with the Greater Flamingo. In addition, he portrays them in a natural setting, far from scientific exhibits of stuffed specimens displayed on perches. Consequently, his birds live, hunt, hatch, peck, fly, and soar.

Barn Swallow

Hirundo rustica
Plate 173
Swallows

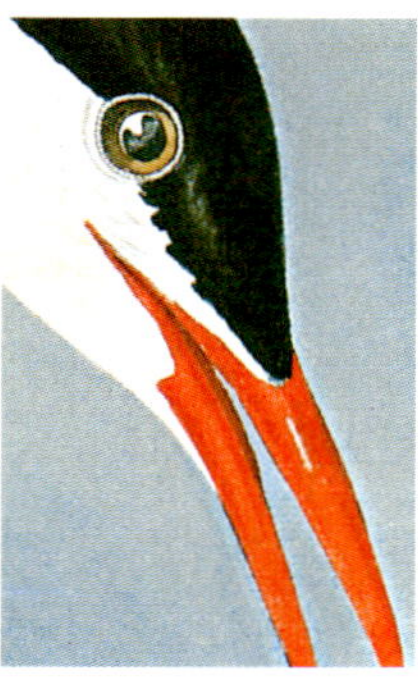

This humanity in representing our environment, in the tradition of Enlightenment thinkers, immediately received its deserved respect in Europe from 1828 onward.

Audubon's impressive oeuvre is composed of two parts: 435 plates, drawn between 1808 and 1838, and 435 notes, *Ornithological Biographies*, later written to accompany the previously published plates. Here again, Audubon exhibited a passion for perfection which pushed him to supervise the colouring and printing of each of the 87,000 requisite plates for the 200 copies of this work.

Artic Tern
———
Sterna paradisaea
Plate 250
Gulls

Finally, the text, including a description of the family, followed by the genus, and finally the species of each bird, is as much a source of scientific information as artistic. Once again, Audubon let the Romantic spirit of his time shine through his work whose harmony and quality are still, if not more than ever, recognised today.

In the following edition, you will find 120 of Audubon's 435 plates in addition to descriptions of the forty five bird families to which he dedicated a lifetime identifying. Therefore, we invite you to discover, thanks to this unprecedented approach, the vanishing universe of this nature lover.

Rose-breasted Grosbeak

Pheucticus ludovicianus
Plate 127
Finches

FAMILY I
Vulturinæ. Vulturine Birds or Vultures

Bill of moderate length, stout, cerate; upper mandible with the tip elongated and decurved; lower mandible rounded and thin-edged at the end. Head rather small, or of moderate size, ovato-oblong, and with part of the neck destitute of feathers. Eyes of moderate size, without projecting ridges.

External aperture of ears rather small and simple. Skin over the fore part of the neck bare or merely downy.

California Condor

Gymnogyps californianus
Plate 426
Vullturine Bird

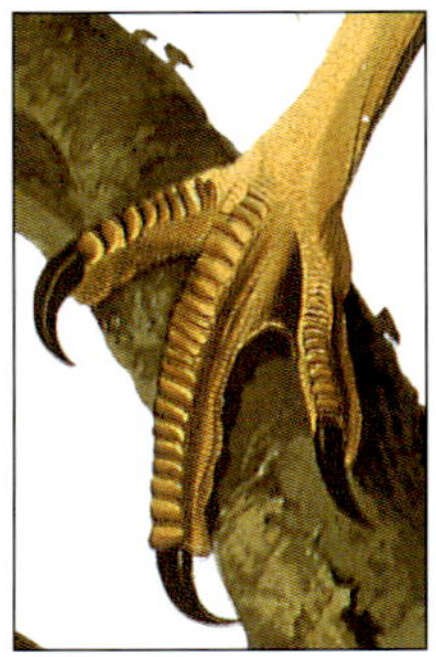

Tarsus rather stout, bare, and shorter than the middle toe, hind toe much smaller than the second; anterior toes connected at the base by a web; claws large, moderately curved, rather acute. Plumage full and rather compact. Wings very long, and subacuminate. Oesophagus excessively wide, and dilated into a crop; stomach rather large, somewhat muscular, with a soft rugous epithelium; intestine of moderate length and width, coeca extremely small. The young when fledged have the head and upper part of the neck generally covered with down. Eggs: commonly two.

Turkey Vulture

Cathartes aura
Plate 151
Vullturine Bird

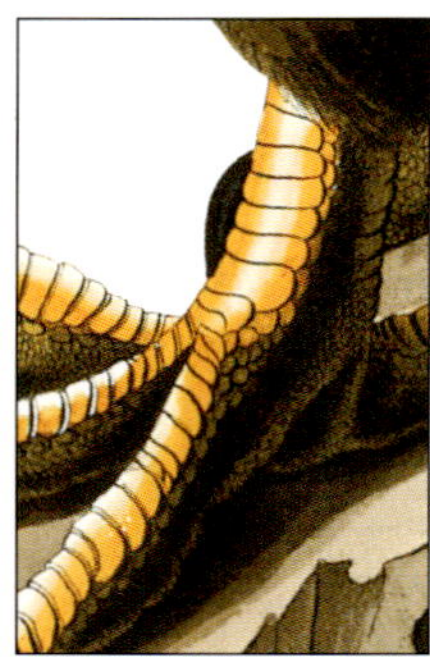

FAMILY II
Falconinæ. Falcons

Bill short, stout, cerate; upper mandible with the tip elongated and decurved; lower mandible rounded and thin edged at the end. Head rather large, broadly ovate, feathered. Eyes large, with prominent superciliary ridges. External aperture of ears of moderate size, and simple. Tarsus longer than the middle toe; claws very large, much curved, extremely acute. Plumage full and generally compact.

Bald Eagle

———

Haliaeetus leucocephalus
Plate 11
Falconine Birds

Wings very long and broad. Oesophagus excessively wide and dilated into a crop; stomach large, membranous, its muscular fasciculi placed in a single series; intestine short and rather wide, or very long and slender. The young, when fledged, generally having their lower parts longitudinally streaked. Eggs: from two to six, ovate, or round. Nest on trees, rocks, or the ground.

Bald Eagle

Haliaeetus leucocephalus
Plate 31
Falconine Birds

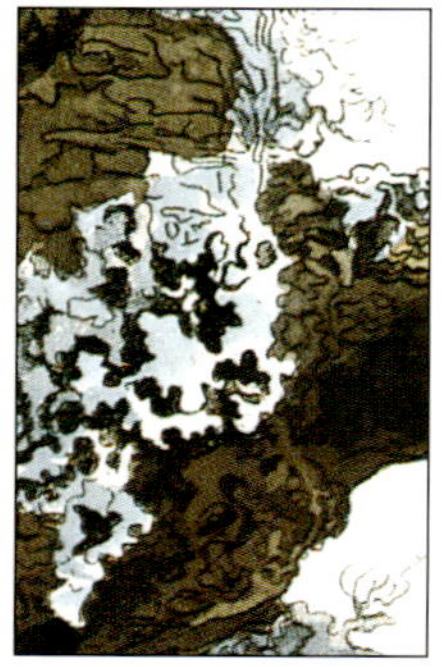

FAMILY III
Striginæ. Owls

Bill very short, strong, cerate; upper mandible with the tip elongated and decurved; lower mandible with the end rounded and thin edged. Head extremely large, owing to the wide separation of the tables of the cranium, rounded, more or less vertically flattened behind, feathered. Eyes excessively large, with prominent superciliary ridges, and encircled by series of decomposed feathers.

Bubo virginianus
Plate 61
Owls

External aperture of ear always very large, frequently excessive, simple or operculate. Tarsus short, very short, or of moderate length, always feathered, as are the toes, of which the outer is versatile, the first shorter than the second, the anterior free; claws very long slender, curved, extremely acute. Plumage very full and soft. Wings long, broad, rounded, the second, third, and fourth quills longest, the filaments of the outer more or less enlarged and recurved at the end.

Great Grey Owl

Strix nebulosa
Plate 351
Owls

Tail broad, rather short or of moderate length, of twelve feathers. Oesophagus very wide, without crop or dilatation; stomach very large, round, membranous, its muscular fasciculi placed in a single series; intestine short and wide. Young at first covered with light coloured down, when fledged, with the face darker than that of adults. Eggs: white, somewhat globular or broadly ovate, from four to six. Nests rudely constructed, in hollow trees, on branches, in buildings, or on the ground.

FAMILY IV
Caprimulginæ. Goatsuckers

Mouth opening to beneath the centre of the eyes; bill much depressed, generally feeble, the horny part being small; upper mandible with the tip somewhat decurved. Nostrils, elliptical, prominent, marginate. Eyes extremely large. Aperture of ear elliptical, very large. Head of extreme breadth, depressed; body very slender. Feet very small; tarsus partially feathered, scaly; anterior toes webbed at the base; hind toe small, and versatile, all scutellate above; claw of third toe generally elongated, with the inner margin thin and pectinate.

Chuck-Willis-Widow

Caprimulgus carolinensis
Plate 52
Goatssuckers

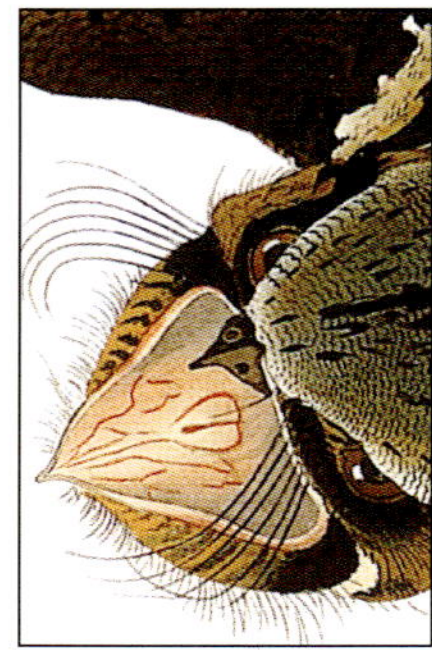

Plumage very soft and blended. Wings very large, the second and third quills longest. Tail long, of ten feathers. Oesophagus rather wide, without crop; stomach very large, rounded, its muscular coat very thin, and composed of a single series of strong fasciculi; epithelium very hard; intestine short and wide. Trachea of nearly uniform width, without inferior laryngeal muscles. Nest on the ground, or in hollow trees. Eggs: generally two. Young covered with down. Very nearly allied in some respects to owls.

Whip-poor-will

Caprimulgus vociferus
Plate 82
Goatssuckers

FAMILY V
Cypselinæ. Swifts

Mouth opening to beneath the hind part of the eyes; bill extremely short, very broad at the base, compressed at the end; upper mandible decurved at the point, the edge inflected, with an indistinct sinus. Nostrils basal, approximate, oblong. Head large and depressed; neck short; body rather slender. Feet extremely short; tarsus rounded, destitute of scutella; toes extremely short, the three anterior nearly equal; hind toe very small, and versatile; claws strong, compressed, arched, very acute.

Chimney Swift

Chaetura pelagica
Plate 158
Swifts

Plumage compact; no bristles at the base of the upper mandible; wings extremely elongated, falciform, the first quill longest; tail of ten feathers. Oesophagus of moderate width, without crop; stomach oblong, moderately muscular, with a dense rugous epithelium; intestine short, and rather wide. No inferior laryngeal muscles. Nest in crevices or holes, or attached to high places. Eggs: elongated, white.

Seaside Sparrow

Ammodramus maritimus
Plate 93
Swallows

FAMILY VI
Hirundinæ. Swallows

Bill very short, much depressed and very broad at the base, compressed toward the tip; upper mandible with the dorsal line convex, the edges overlapping, with a small notch close to the slightly decurved tip. Head broad, depressed; neck very short, body moderate. Feet very short, tarsus very short, anteriorly scutellate; toes of moderate size; first large, all scutellate in their whole length; claws rather strong, compressed, well curved, acute. Plumage soft, blended, glossy.

Marsh Wren

Cistothorus palustris
Plate 100
Swallows

No bristles at the base of the bill. Wings extremely long, narrow, pointed, somewhat falciform; secondaries very short. Tail generally emarginate, of twelve feathers. Mouth extremely wide; oesophagus rather wide, without crop; stomach elliptical or rounded, muscular, with a dense rugous epithelium. Four pairs of inferior laryngeal muscles. Nest in holes in banks, buildings, or trees, or attached to the surface of these objects. Eggs: from four to six, white, plain, or spotted.

Purple Martin

Progne subis
Plate 22
Swallows

FAMILY VII
Muscicapinæ. Flycatchers

Bill depressed, triangular, compressed at the end, upper mandible notched, lower with the point slightly ascending. Head rather large, depressed; neck short; body rather slender. Feet generally short; tarsus short, slender, with very broad scutella. Toes: four, free; the hind toe not proportionally large; claws arched, compressed, and acute. Plumage soft and blended; wings long, with the first quill generally long, the outer three longest. Tail various.

Fork-tailed Flycatcher

Tyrannus savana
Plate 168
Flycatchers

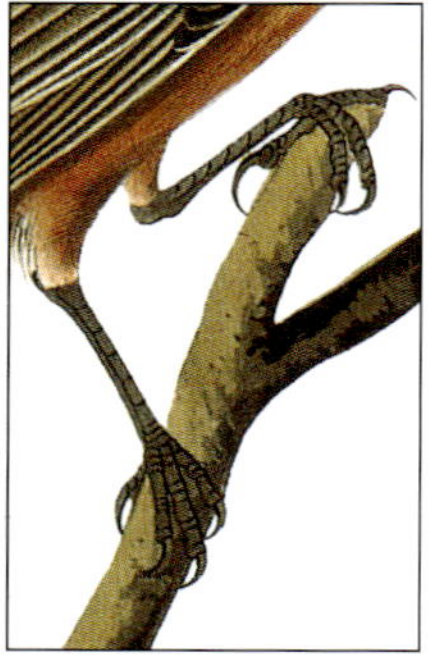

Tongue flattened, sagittate, bristly at the tip, oesophagus wide, without crop; stomach elliptical, moderately muscular, with the lateral muscles distinct, the epithelium thin, dense, longitudinally rugous; intestine short. Trachea simple, inferior laryngeal muscles, forming on each side a large pad, but not divisible into several portions as in the singing birds. Nests regularly formed, cup-shaped. Eggs from four to six.

FAMILY VIII
Sylvicolinæ. Wood Warblers

Bill short or of moderate length, rather slender and conical, considerably broader than high at the base, gradually compressed toward the end. Upper mandible with its dorsal outline straight until near the end, the point very narrow, the notches very slight. Lower mandible with the angle rather short and narrow, the dorsal line straight, the edges somewhat involute, the tip acute.

Canada Warbler

Wilsonia canadensis
Plate 5
Wood Warblers

Head moderate, ovate; neck short; body rather slender. Feet of moderate length; tarsus longer than the middle toe, slender, much compressed, with eight anterior scutella, of which the upper are blended; toes rather small, or of moderate size, bind toe proportionally stout, outer adherent for a short way at the base; claws moderate, much compressed, arched, acute. Plumage generally soft and blended. Wings of moderate length.

Parula americana
Plate 15
Wood Warblers

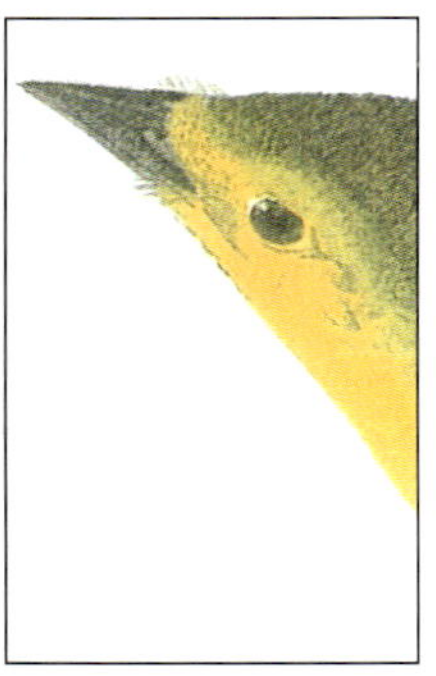

Tail of moderate length, of twelve feathers. Tongue of moderate length, sagittate, tapering. Oesophagus of moderate width, without dilatation, proventriculus bulbiform; stomach of moderate size, rounded or elliptical, moderately muscular, with the muscles distinct; epithelium dense, longitudinally rugous; intestine short, rather wide. Trachea simple; with four pairs of inferior laryngeal muscles.

Hooded Warbler

Wilsonia citrina
Plate 9
Wood Warblers

FAMILY IX
Certhianæ. Creepers

Bill of moderate length or rather long, slender, slightly arched, much compressed, acute; upper mandible with its dorsal outline convex or arched, the ridge narrow, the notches slight or obsolete, lower mandible with the angle rather long and narrow, the dorsal line straight or slightly decurved, the edges inclinate, the tip acute. Head moderate, ovate; neck short.

Trogrodytes aedon
Plate 83
Creepers

Body slender. Feet of moderate length, or rather short; tarsus about the same length as the middle toe, compressed, with eight anterior scutella, toes of moderate length and much compressed, hind toe proportionally long, outer adherent at the base; claws rather long, extremely compressed, arched, and acute. Wings short or of moderate length. Tail of twelve feathers, generally much rounded.

Carolina Wren

Thryothorus ludovicianus
Plate 78
Creepers

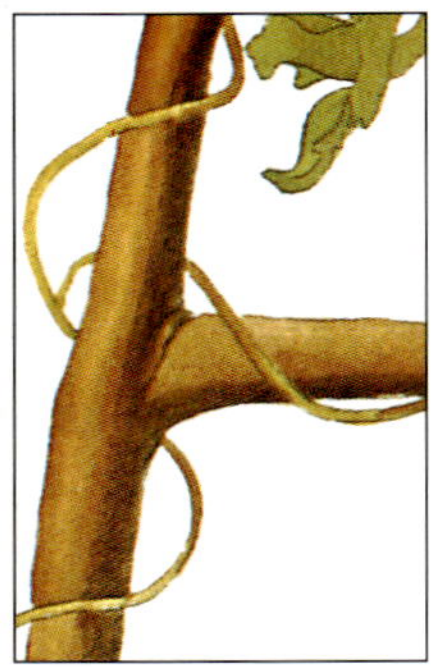

Tongue slender, emarginate and papillate at the base, very narrow, tapering to a lacerated point. Oesophagus of moderate width, without crop; proventriculus bulbiform; stomach of moderate size, oblong, or elliptical, moderately muscular, with the muscles distinct; epithelium dense, longitudinally rugous; intestine short, rather wide. Trachea simple, with four pairs of inferior laryngeal muscles.

Boreal Chickadee

Parus hudsonicus
Plate 194
Tits

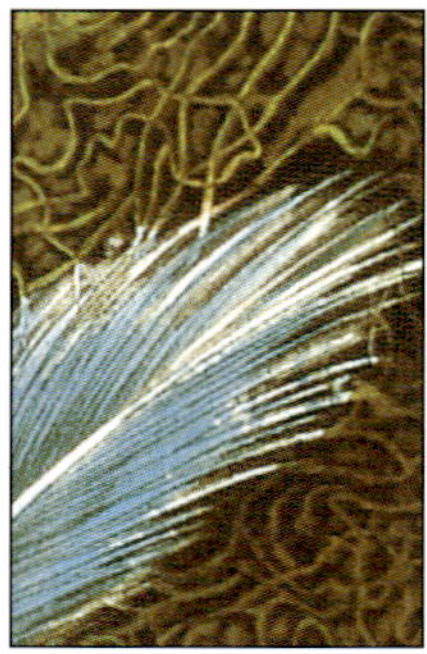

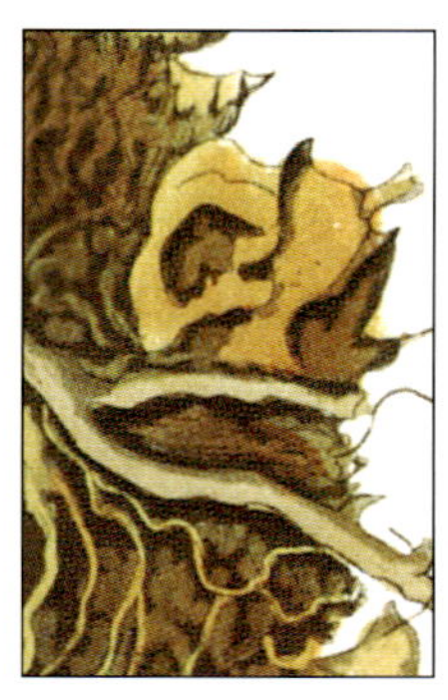

FAMILY X
Parinæ. Tits

Bill very short or of moderate length, straight, strong, compressed, rather sharp; both mandible with the dorsal line sloping and slightly convex, the sides convex, the edges sharp; notches obsolete. Nostrils basal, round, concealed by the feathers. Head rather large, round; neck short; body short, and rather full.

Feet of moderate length, rather stout tarsus rather short, compressed, with eight, distinct scutella; toes large, the three anterior united as far as the second joint, the hind toe much stronger and flattened beneath; claws rather long, stout, arched, much compressed, acute.

Bushtit, Black-Capped Chickadee
and Chestnut-Backed Chickadee

———————————————————

Psaltriparus minimus, Parus atricapillus, Parus rufescens
Plate 353
Tits

Plumage very soft, blended, and full. Feathers at the base of the bill directed forwards. Wings of moderate length, much rounded, with the first quill very small, the fourth and fifth longest. Tail rather long, slender, of twelve narrow rounded feathers. Tongue emarginate and papillate at the base, abrupt at the tip, with four bristles. Oesophagus narrow, without dilatation; proventriculus oblong; stomach a rather strong oblong gizzard, with the muscles distinct, the epithelium dense, thin, longitudinally rugous; intestine short, of moderate width. Trachea simple, with four pairs of inferior laryngeal muscles.

Parus bicolor
Plate 39
Tits

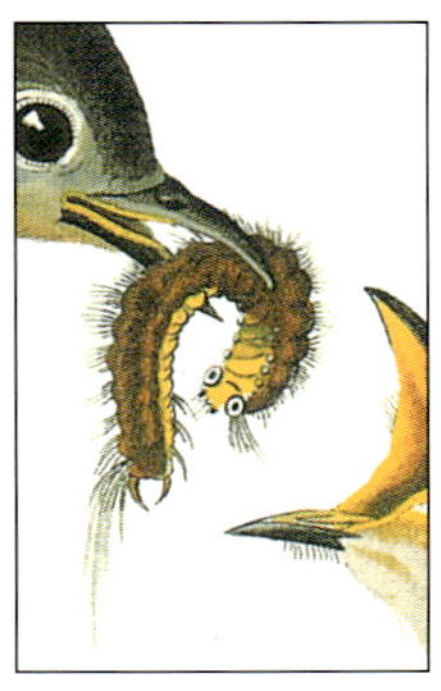

FAMILY XI
Sylvianæ. Warblers

Bill of moderate length, slender, straight, a little broader than high at the base, compressed toward the end; upper mandible with its dorsal line straight and declinate, convex at the end, the tip small, acute, the notches small; lower mandible with the angle of moderate length and narrow, the dorsal line straight, the sides convex, the tip narrow. Nostrils basal, oval or oblong.

Head rather large, ovate; neck short; body rather slender. Feet of ordinary length, slender; tarsus compressed, with seven anterior scutella; toes moderate, compressed;

Eastern Bluebird

Sialia sialis
Plate 113
Warblers

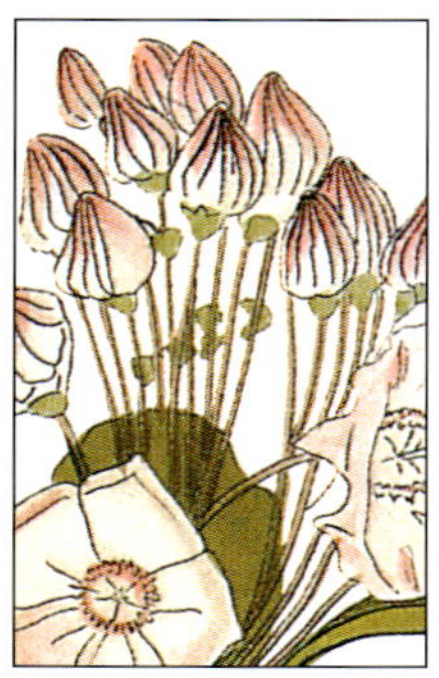

first stouter, second and fourth nearly equal, third much longer, and adherent at the base; claws moderate, arched, slender, compressed, acute. Plumage soft and blended. Bristles short or weak. Wings of moderate length or long, the first quill very small, the second, third, and fourth longest. Tail long or of moderate length, of twelve feathers. Tongue, sagittate, slender, tapering to a slit and lacerated point. Oesophagus rather narrow, without crop; proventriculus oblong;

Regulus civieri
Plate 55
Warblers

stomach a gizzard of moderate strength, with the muscles distinct, the epithelium dense and rugous; intestine of moderate length.

Trachea simple, with four pairs of inferior laryngeal muscles.

Of this family, which in Europe is so numerous, there are in North America only two genera, Regulus and Sialia, the former composed of very small birds, allied in manner to the Tits, the latter approaching the Thrushes in form. The connecting links being wanting, these genera might seem, at first sight, very dissimilar.

Ruby-Crowned Kinglet

Regulus calendula
Plate 195
Warblers

FAMILY XII
Turdinæ. Thrushes

Bill short, or of moderate length, rather strong, straight, compressed toward the end; upper mandible with its dorsal outline a little convex and declinate, the tip small, rather acute, the notches small; lower mandible with the angle rather short, of moderate width, the dorsal line straight, the sides convex, the tip acute. Head oblong, compressed, of moderate size; neck rather short: body moderate.

American Goldfinch

Carduelis tristis
Plate 33
Thrushes

Eyes of moderate size. External aperture of ear is large and round. Feet of moderate strength; tarsus compressed, with seven anterior scutella; toes rather strong, compressed; first, second, and fourth, nearly equal, third much longer, and adherent to the fourth at the base; claws rather long, arched, compressed, laterally grooved, and acute. Plumage rather blended. Bristles small.

Northern Mockingbird

Mimus polyglottos
Plate 21
Thrushes

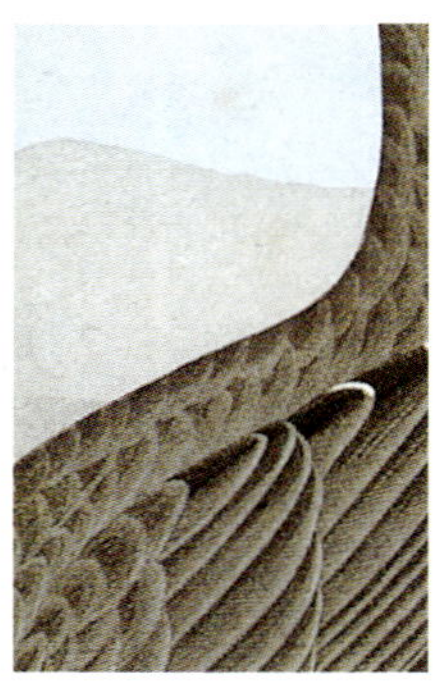

Wings of moderate length, broad, rounded; the first quill very small, third and fourth longest. Tail of twelve feathers, varying in length. Tongue sagittate and papillate at the base, slender, tapering, its tip slit. Oesophagus rather narrow, without crop; proventriculus oblong; stomach a gizzard of moderate strength, its lateral and lower muscles distinct; the epithelium dense and rugous; intestine of moderate length. Trachea simple, with four pairs of inferior laryngeal muscles.

American Dipper

Cinclus mexicanus
Plate 370
Thrushes

FAMILY XIII
Motacillinæ. Wagtails

Bill of moderate length, straight, slender, a little broader than high at the base, compressed toward the end; upper mandible with the dorsal line sloping, a little convex toward the end, the nostrils slight, the tip acute; lower mandible with the angle rather large and narrow, the dorsal line ascending and scarcely convex, the edges somewhat involute, the tip acute.

Witer Pipit

Anthus spinoletta
Plate 80
Wagtails

General form slender; head ovato-oblong; neck short. Feet of ordinary length, slender; toes very slender, the lateral equal, the outer adherent at the base, the hind toe rather large; claws rather long, arched, compressed; acute, that of the hind toe generally very long. Plumage soft and blended. Bristles small. Wings long and pointed, one of the minor secondaries often much elongated and tapering.

Seiurus aurocapillus
Plate 143
Wagtails

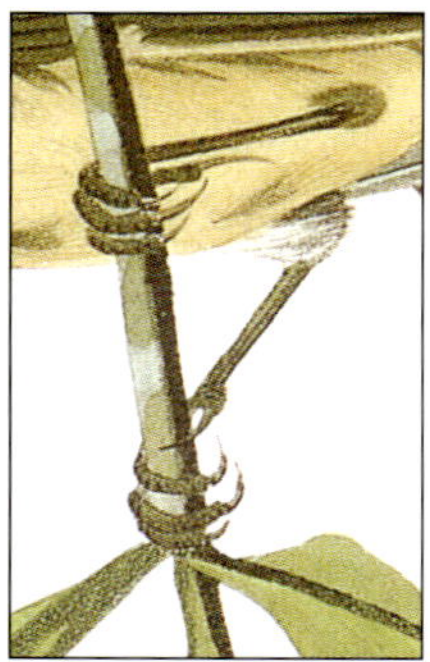

Tongue sagittate, slender, with the tip slit; oesophagus uniform; stomach a very muscular gizzard, rounded, with large tendons, and thin rugous epithelium; intestine of moderate length. Trachea simple, with four pairs of inferior laryngeal muscles. This family is connected with the Turdinae by Seiurus, and with the Alandinae by Anthus, which are the only two American genera.

FAMILY XIV
Alaudinæ. Larks

Bill rather short, or of moderate length, somewhat conical, compressed toward the end. Upper mandible dorsal line sloping and slightly convex, the edges sharp and overlapping, the notches generally obsolete; the tip narrow and a little deflected; lower mandible of moderate length and narrow, the dorsal line ascending and nearly straight, the edges slightly inflected, the tip acute; gape-line straight. Nostrils elliptical or oblong, basal.

Horned Lark

Eremophila alpestris
Plate 200
Larks

Head oblong, of moderate size neck rather short; body ovate. Feet of moderate length, or rather long; tarsus compressed, with eight anterior scutella; toes slender, compressed; the hind toe elongated, second and fourth about equal, third much longer. Claws rather long, arched, slender, much compressed, laterally grooved, acute, that of the hind toe very long, straight, tapering. Plumage generally soft and blended. Wings rather long, broad, the inner secondaries tapering, and one so elongated as nearly to equal the longest primary, when the wing is closed.

Western Tanager and Scarlet Tanager

Piranga ludoviciana, Piranga olivacea
Plate 354
Finches

Tail of twelve feathers, generally emarginate. Roof of the upper mandible concave, generally with three prominent lines; tongue slender, thin, flat, tapering to a slit and bristly tip; oesophagus of uniform width; stomach a very strong muscular gizzard of a rounded form and compressed, its lateral muscles very large, its epithelium dense and rugous; intestines short, of moderate width. Nest on the ground. Eggs – five or six, oval, spotted.

Black-Headed Grosbeak and Evening Grosbeak

Pheucticus melanocephalus, Coccothraustes vespertinus, Hesperiphona verspertina
Plate 373
Finches

FAMILY XV
Fringillinæ. Finches

Bill short, stout, conical, acute; upper mandible generally with its dorsal line more or less convex, the sides rounded, the edges inflected or direct, the tip acute; lower mandible with the dorsal line ascending and slightly convex, the edges involute. Gape-line ascending for more than a quarter of its length, then direct. Nostrils basal, round, partly concealed by feathers.

Rufous-Sided Towhee or Eastern Towhee

Pipilo erythrophthalmus
Plate 29
Finches

Head of moderate size, or rather large, ovate or rounded; neck short; body compact; tarsus generally shorter than the middle toe with its claw, compressed, with seven or eight anterior scutella; hind toe stout; outer toe adherent at the base, lateral about equal. Claws large or moderate, compressed, laterally grooved, acute. Plumage soft and blended, but firm. Wings various, acute, or rounded. Tail of twelve feathers. Roof of upper mandible concave, with three prominent lines, of which the middle is sometimes elevated into an oblong hard prominence.

Savannah Sparrow

Passerculus sandwichensis
Plate 109
Finches

Tongue much compressed, pointed; oesophagus rather wide, with a dilatation or crop on the right side; stomach round or oblong, muscular, with the epithelium, thin, dense, and longitudinally rugous; intestine short, rather wide. Trachea simple, with four pairs of inferior laryngeal muscles. The Fringilline pass into the Icterine on the one hand, and the Alaudinae on the other. The Buntings scarcely differ from the Finches in any other character than the knob on the palate, which is common to them with the Icterinae.

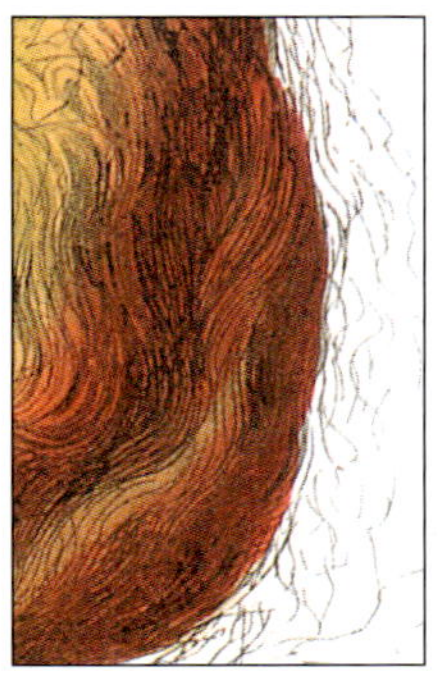

FAMILY XVI
Agelainæ. Marsh Blackbirds

Bill of moderate length, sometimes short, seldom longer than the head, stout, straight, conical, compressed, tapering, pointed. The upper mandible with the dorsal line nearly straight, the nasal sinus short and very wide, the ridge thus appearing to encroach on the forehead, the sides rounded, the edges without notch; lower mandible with the angle short and rounded, the dorsal line straight, the edges involute.

Common grackle

Quiscalus quiscula
Plate 7
Marsh Blackbirds

Nostrils basal, round or oblong. Head rather large, ovate; neck short; body moderately full. Legs of moderate length, stout, rather slender; tarsus compressed, with eight anterior scutella; hind toe large, lateral toes equal, the outer adherent at the base. Claws generally large, arched, compressed, acute. Plumage soft, blended, in the males usually glossy.

Boat-Tailed Grackle

Quiscalus major
Plate 187
Marsh Blackbirds

Wings of moderate length, with the outer three or four quills longest, the first being very little shorter than the second, or sometimes even exceeding it: tail of twelve feathers, of moderate length, or elongated. The roof of the upper mandible concave, with three longitudinal ridges, of which the middle is larger, and at the base forms a hard prominence: tongue sagittate and papillate at the base, narrow, deep, pointed.

Oesophagus wider dilated about the middle proventriculus oblong; stomach rounded or elliptical, with the lateral muscles distinct and well developed; the epithelium dense and longitudinally rugous; intestine short. Trachea simple, with four pairs of inferior laryngeal muscles. Female much smaller. Nests variously on trees or bushes, or on the ground, generally elaborate. Eggs – about five, ovate, spotted and streaked.

Orchard Oriole

Icterus spurius
Plate 42
Marsh Blackbirds

FAMILY XVII
Sturninæ. Starlings

Bill nearly as long as the head, moderately stout, or rather slender, nearly straight, compressed toward the end. The upper mandible with its outline straight, slightly convex toward the tip, the ridge somewhat flattened, the sides sloping and convex, the edges sharp and overlapping, with a very slight or obsolete notch, close to the depressed tip.

Eastern Meadowlark

Sturnella magna
Plate 136
Starlings

The lower mandible with the angle long and rather acute, the crura rather broad and flat at the base, the dorsal line straight, the edges sharp, the tip slender; gape-line ascending gently at the base, then direct. Head ovate or oblong, flattened above; neck of moderate length; body rather full. Feet moderately stout; tarsus rather short, compressed, with seven anterior scutella; toes moderate, or rather long, the first stouter, the lateral toes equal, the outer adherent at the base. Claws rather long, moderately arched, compressed, acute. Plumage rather compact.

Cyanocitta cristata
Plate 102
Crows

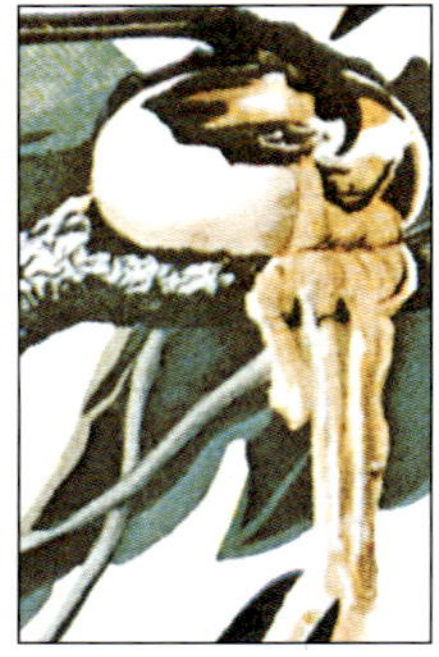

Wings of moderate length, with the first quill very small, the third and fourth longest. Tail short or of moderate length, rounded, and generally emarginate. Roof of upper mandible with a median ridge; tongue slender, thin-edged, with the tip slit and lacerated; oesophagus without dilatation; stomach round, its muscular coat rather thin, the epithelium dense, and longitudinally rugous; intestine of moderate length and width. Trachea simple, with four pairs of inferior laryngeal muscles. Nests on the ground, or in cavities; eggs – about five.

Blue Jay

Cyanocitta cristata
Plate 102
Crows

FAMILY XVIII
Corvinæ. Crows

Bill about the length of the head, robust, nearly straight, and compressed: upper mandible with the dorsal line more or less arched, its tip slightly deflected, the edges sharp, with a slight notch or sinus. Nostrils basal, round, concealed by stiff slender reversed feathers. Head rather large, ovate; neck of moderate length, body compact.

American Crow

Corvus brachyrhynchos
Plate 156
Crows

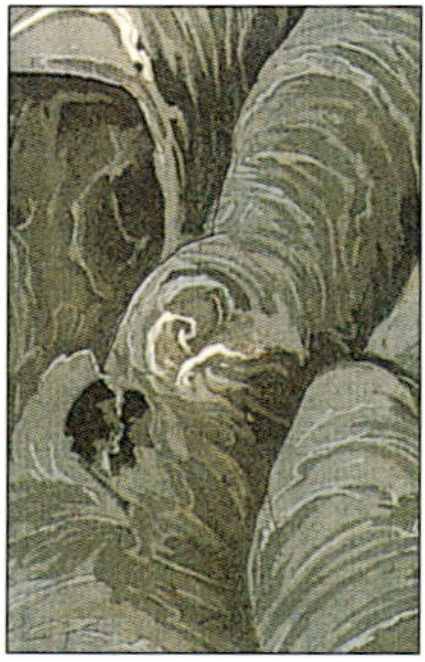

Feet of ordinary length, rather stout: tarsus compressed, with about eight large scutella; toes four, first stronger, but about the same length as the second and fourth, which latter is adherent at the base. Claws rather large, arched, compressed, acute. Plumages various, wings long or of moderate length, much rounded, the first quill about half the length of the fourth or fifth, which are longest. Tail of twelve broad feathers.

Gray Jay

Perisoreus canadensis
Plate 107
Crows

Upper mandible concave, with several longitudinal ridges; tongue oblong, flat above, horny, thin edged, with the tip slit and lacerated; oesophagus of moderate width, without dilatation; proventriculus bulbiform; stomach, a gizzard of moderate power, with a rugous dense epithelium; intestine of moderate length and width. Trachea with four pairs of inferior laryngeal muscles. Nests in high places, or in cavities, rudely constructed. Eggs - from four to six, ovate or oblong.

Common Raven

Corvus corax
Plate 101
Crows

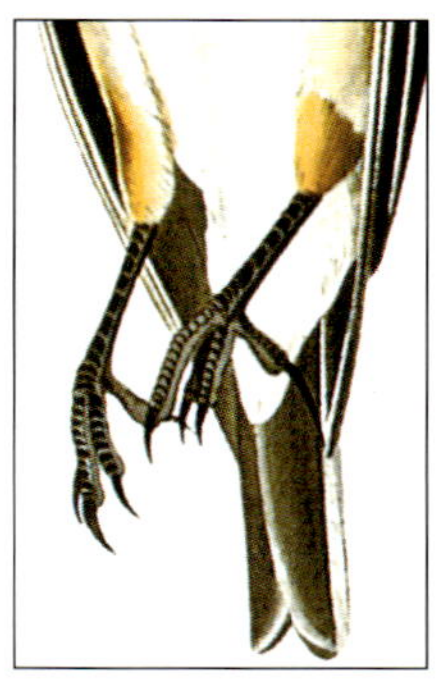

FAMILY XIX
Laninæ. Shrikes

Bill short, or of moderate length, stout, broader than high at the base, compressed toward the end; the gape-line slightly arched, the ridge narrow, the notch and dentiform process large, the tip narrow and decurved. Head large, round, ovate; neck short; body compact. Legs of moderate length; tarsus compressed, with seven anterior scutella; toes moderate, compressed; hind toe rather stout, lateral about equal, the outer adherent at the base. Claws arched, compressed, acute.

Northern Shrike

Lanius excubitor
Plate 192
Shrikes

Plumage soft and blended. Bristles rather strong. Wings and tail various. Roof of upper mandible narrow, with a median ridge; tongue slender, toward the end, with the margins lacerated, and the tip slit; oesophagus wide, uniform proventriculus elliptical; stomach broadly elliptical or rounded; its muscular coat thin, the epithelium dense and longitudinally rugous; intestine of moderate length. Trachea simple; four pairs of inferior laryngeal muscles.

Loggerhead Shrike

Lanius ludovicianus
Plate 57
Shrikes

FAMILY XX
Vireoninæ. Greenlets

Bill of moderate length, straight, rather stout, compressed toward the end; gape-line slightly arched, notches distinct, tip very small, declinate. Head rather large, ovate; neck short; body rather slender. Feet of moderate length; tarsus compressed, slender, with seven anterior scutella; toes rather small, hind toe rather stout, lateral equal. Claws moderate, arched, compressed, acute. Plumage soft and blended.

Yellow Throated Vireo

Vireo flavifrons
Plate 119
Greenlets

Wings of moderate length, rather pointed. Tail of moderate length, even or emarginate. Roof of upper mandible concave, with a median ridge; tongue narrow, flat above, with the point slit; oesophagus of moderate length and without dilatation; stomach, round, muscular, with a dense rugous epithelium; intestine short, and rather wide. Trachea simple, with four pairs of inferior laryngeal muscles.

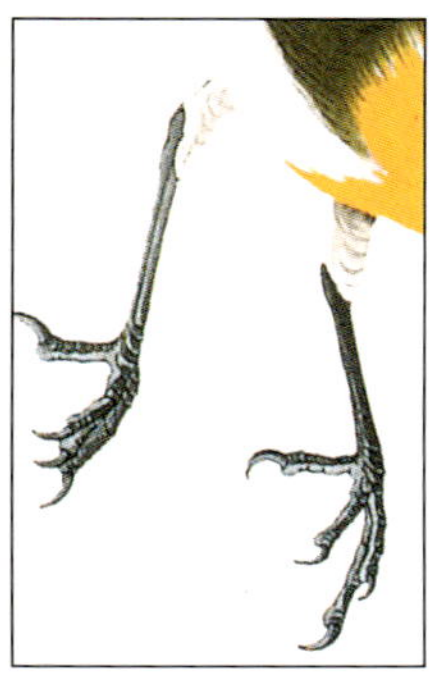

FAMILY XXI
Piprinæ. Manakins

Bill short, stout, straight, depressed, being much broader than high at the base, with the dorsal line arched, the ridge narrow, the sides sloping, the gape-line straight or slightly arched, the notches rather large, the tip very small and declinate. Head rather large, broadly ovate; neck short; body compact. Tarsus of moderate length, compressed, with seven anterior scutella; toes small, the hind one not much stouter, the lateral equal. Claws moderate, arched, compressed, acute.

Plumage soft, and blended. Wings of moderate length, broad, and rounded. Tail short or of moderate length, generally rounded. Roof of upper mandible concave, with a prominent median line; tongue triangular, horny, thin-edged, rather obtuse, bristly at the end; oesophagus wide, without dilatation; stomach rather small, moderately muscular, with a dense rugous epithelium; intestine short, of moderate width.

Cardinalis cardinalis
Plate 159
Finches

FAMILY XXII
Ampelinæ. Chatterers

Bill short, depressed, rather weak, triangular when viewed from above, compressed at the end, its upper outline arched, the gape-line nearly straight, the notches very small, the tip very small and declinate. Nostrils elliptical, partially concealed by reversed bristly feathers. Head ovate; neck short; and body moderate or full. Feet short; tarsus short, rather stout, compressed; toes rather small. Claws rather long, arched, much compressed, acute.

Bohemian Waxwing

Bombycilla garrulus
Plate 363
Chatterers

Plumage generally blended and glossy. Wings of moderate length, broad. Tail short or of moderate length. Roof of upper mandible rather concave, with three longitudinal ridges; tongue horny, deeply slit; oesophagus very wide, dilated about the middle; stomach small, elliptical, moderately muscular; intestine of moderate length and very wide. Trachea simple, with four pairs of very small inferior laryngeal muscles.

Cedar Waxwing

Bombycilla cedrorum
Plate 43
Chatterers

FAMILY XXIII
Sittinæ. Nut Hatches

Bill of moderate length or rather long, straight, slender, conico-subulate, somewhat compressed, with the tips acute or cuneate. Head ovate; neck short; body full. Tarsi rather short, or of moderate length, slender, compressed, with seven or eight scutella; toes long, very slender; hind toe extremely long; anterior little spreading; claws long, little arched, slender, much compressed, acute. Plumage soft and full.

White-breasted Nuthatch

Sitta carolinensis
Plate 152
Nut Hatches

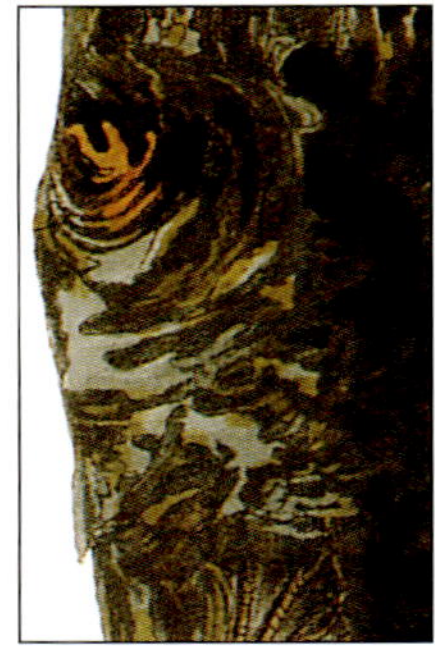

Wings of moderate length, broad, rounded. Tail short, broad, of twelve feathers. Roof of upper mandible very narrow, slightly concave, with three ridges; tongue very slender, with the tip abrupt and bristly; oesophagus without dilatation; stomach round, moderately muscular; intestine short and wide. Trachea simple; with a single pair of large inferior laryngeal muscles. Allied to the Titmice on the one hand, and the Woodpeckers on the other.

Brown-Headed Nuthatch

Sitta pusilla
Plate 125
Nut Hatches

FAMILY XXIV
Trochilinæ. Humming Birds

Bill long, very slender, straight or arched, somewhat depressed at the base, subcylindrical, flexible, acute. Head rather large; neck of moderate length; body moderately robust. Feet very short, rather stout tarsus extremely short; toes of moderate size; the anterior coherent at the base, and nearly of equal length, the hind toe articulated high on the tarsus; claws rather long, arched, much compressed, very acute.

Ruby Throated Hummingbird

Archilochus colubris
Plate 47
Humming Birds

Plumage compact above, soft and blended beneath, often with metallic lustre ; wings very long, extremely narrow, falciform, with the first quill longest, the other primaries rapidly diminishing; secondaries extremely short. Tail various, of ten feathers. Tongue very long, slender, with two flat, thin-edged terminal filaments, and extensile by means of the elongation of the hyoid bones, which curve over the head to the fore part of the forehead, and with their muscles slide in groove, like those of the Woodpeckers.

Black Throated Mango

Anthracothorax nigricollis
Plate 184
Humming Birds

Oesophagus narrow, considerably enlarged about the middle; stomach extremely small, round, moderately muscular, its epithelium dense and longitudinally rugous; intestine very short and of moderate width. Trachea simple, but divided very high up on the neck, so that the bronchi are of excessive length, with a pair of inferior laryngeal muscles.

Sepasphorus rufus
Plate 379
Humming Birds

FAMILY XXV
Alcedinæ. Kingfishers

Bill long, straight, stout, broader than high at the base, much compressed, tapering to a rather acute point, and gape line commencing beneath the middle of the eyes. Head large, ovato-oblong, neck short, and body stout. Tarsus extremely short; anteriorly scaly; anterior toes united for more than half their length, outer longer than inner, hind toe small claws stout, compressed, arched, very acute. Plumage rather compact. Wings rather long, pointed. Tail various, of twelve feathers.

Belted Kingfisher

Ceryle alcyon
Plate 77
Kingfishers

Tongue very short, fleshy, with its sides parallel, the tip tapering to a blunt point. Roof of upper mandible moderately concave, with a median ridge and oblique lateral grooves. Oesophagus very wide, without crop; stomach very large, round, with its muscular coat very thin; the epithelium dense, very thin, with tortuous rugae; intestine very long, extremely slender; cloaca very large, globular. Trachea with three pairs of inferior laryngeal muscles.

FAMILY XXVI
Picinæ. Woodpeckers

Bill long or of moderate length, straight, stout, angular, tapering, compressed toward the tip, which is generally wedge shaped and abrupt; mandibles nearly equal, outline of the tipper slightly convex, the ridge narrow, sides sloping, with a lateral ridge, edges straight; lower with the angle short and narrow, the dorsal line nearly straight, the ridge narrow, the sides with a faint ridge.

Yellow Bellied Sapsucker

Sphyrapicus varius
Plate 190
Woodpeckers

Nostrils basal, elliptical or oblong, concealed by reversed bristly feathers. Head of moderate size and oblong, neck of moderate length and body stout. Legs short, tarsus short and moderately stout, anteriorly scutellate, scaly behind. Toes usually four, first short, rudimentary, or sometimes wanting, fourth very large and reversed, equalling or exceeding the third. Claws large, strong, much curved, much compressed, very acute.

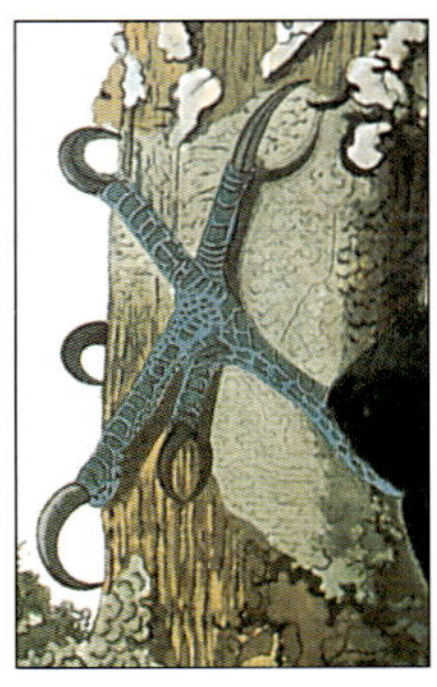

Ivory Billed Woodpecker

Campephilus principalis
Plate 66
Woodpeckers

Plumage soft, blended, rather compact at the back; wings of moderate length or long; with the first quill very small, the third, fourth, and fifth longest. Tail of moderate length, much rounded or cuneate, of twelve feathers, of which the lateral are extremely small, and placed above the next, the rest, but especially the three middle pairs, with the shafts exceedingly large and strong, the webs narrowed toward the end, their filaments deflected and stiff, the tip pointed or emarginate from being worn.

Three-toed Woodpecker and Hairy Woodpecker

Picoides tridactylus, Picoides villosus
Plate 417
Woodpeckers

Tongue slender, with the tip horny and furnished with reversed prickles or bristles, capable of being protruded to a great length by the elongation of the hyoid bones, which curve over the head to between the right eye and nostril, or even extend round a great part of that eye. Oesophagus of uniform width; proventriculus extremely large; stomach of moderate size, or rather small,

broadly elliptical or rounded, moderately muscular; epithelium thin, dense, and longitudinally rugous; intestine of moderate length, rather wide; cloaca very large, globular, or elliptical. Trachea simple, with a single pair of inferior laryngeal muscles. Nest is a cavity dug in a tree; eggs from four to six, elliptical, white.

The groups present characters that are so undecided, and exhibit such gradual approximations, that I think it better here to consider all our Woodpeckers as of one genus.

FAMILY XXVII
Cuculinæ. Cuckoos

Bill long or of moderate length, broader than high at the base, compressed toward the end, straight or somewhat arched. Upper mandible with the dorsal line convex or arched, the ridge indistinct, the sides convex, the edges arched, sharp, without notch, the tip decurved; lower mandible with the angle rather short, the dorsal lines straight or decurved, the ridge thin, the sides erect or convex, the tip slightly decurved, acute. Nostrils basal, oblong, generally marginate.

Mangrove Cockoo

Coccyzus minor
Plate 169
Cuckoos

Head of moderate size; neck of ordinary length; body rather slender. Feet of moderate length; tarsus with broad scutella; toes long, slender, flat beneath, outer directed outwards or backwards. Claws long or of moderate length, arched, compressed, acute. Plumage blended; wings generally large, with the fixed quill short, the third and fourth longest.

Yellow-Billed Cuckoo

Coccyzus americanus
Plate 2
Cuckoos

Tail long, of ten feathers; upper mandible very narrow beneath, with three longitudinal ridges; tongue slender, emarginate, and papillate at the base, the tip horny, thin, lacerated, and slit; oesophagus rather wide, without dilatation; stomach large, round, with the muscular coat very thin, the epithelium soft, rugous; intestine of moderate length and width. Trachea simple, with a single very slender pair of inferior laryngeal muscles.

Black-billed Cuckoo

Cuccyzus erythropthalmus
Plate 32
Cuckoos

FAMILY XXVIII
Psittacinæ. Parrots

Bill short, bulging, very strong, deeper than broad, convex above and below; upper mandible cerate at the base, its outline decurved, the sides convex, the edges sharp, with an angular process, the tip trigonal, decurved, elongated, acute; lower mandible with the angle short and wide, the tip thin-edged, rounded, or abrupt. Nostrils basal, round, open in the cere. Head very large; neck of moderate length; body compact.

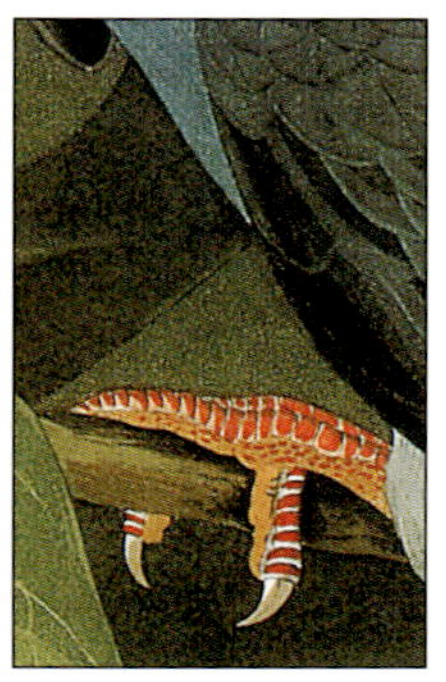

Feet short and robust; tarsus short, scaly; toes stout, the outer directed backwards, the third and fourth coherent at the base. Claws stout, curved, acute. Plumage generally blended, but firm. Wings and tail various. Tongue short, fleshy, rounded, or emarginate; oesophagus wide, with a large crop; stomach small, muscular; intestine of moderate length; cloaca globular.

White-crowned Pigeon

Comumba leucocephala
Plate 177
Pigeons

FAMILY XXIX
Columbinæ. Pigeons

Bill short, soft for half its length, horny toward the end. Upper mandible with a tumid fleshy covering at the base, its dorsal line straight, toward the end convex and deflected, the tip narrow, but obtuse; lower mandible at its base wider than the upper, its sides elastic and slender, the angle long and obtuse, the dorsal line short and convex, the tip obtuse. Nostrils linear in the lower and fore part of the nasal membrane. Head small and oblong, neck of moderate length, body rather full.

Passenger Pigeon

Ectopistes mogratorius
Plate 62
Pigeons

Feet short; tarsus partially feathered, scutellate, or scaly; toes four, on the same level, broad beneath, marginate; the first short, the lateral nearly equal, all scutellate above. Claws moderate, arched, compressed, rather blunt. Plumage generally compact, the feathers with thick spongy shaft, and destitute of plumule. Wings and tail various. Tongue rather broad at the base, toward the end narrow, horny, induplicate, pointed; oesophagus very wide, enlarged into an enormous crop; stomach a very large and strong gizzard, placed obliquely,

Zeneida Dove

Zeneida aurita
Plate 162
Pigeons

its lateral muscles exceedingly thick, the lower prominent, the tendons very large, the epithelium dense, with longitudinal broad rugae, and two opposite grinding surfaces; intestine long, of moderate width; cloaca oblong. Trachea simple, flattened, with a single pair of inferior laryngeal muscles. Nest flat, rudely constructed. Eggs two, elliptical, white.

Band-Tailed Pigeon

Columba fasciata
Plate 367
Pigeons

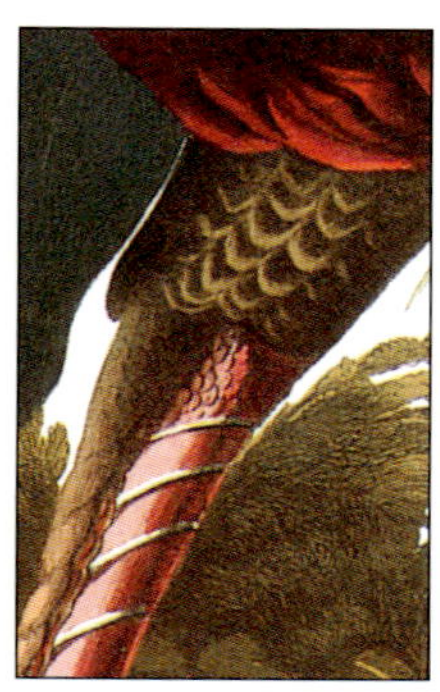

FAMILY XXX
Pavoninæ. Pavonine Birds

Bill rather short, moderately stout, broader than high at the base, somewhat compressed toward the end; upper mandible with its extremity arched, thin-edged, and obtuse; lower narrowed and blunt. Head partially denuded and rather small, oblong neck long, body very large. Feet stout, rather long; tarsus anteriorly scutellate; hind toe elevated, much developed. Wings of moderate length, convex, rounded. Tail very large, of more than twelve feathers.

Wild Turkey

Meleagris gallopavo
Plate 1
Pavonine Birds

Tongue triangular, pointed; oesophagus dilated into an enormous crop; stomach a very powerful gizzard, rounded or transversely elliptical with very large muscles, and dense epithelium, having two concave grinding surfaces; intestines large, and rather wide. Trachea cylindrical, with out inferior laryngeal muscles. Nest on the ground, rudely constructed. Eggs numerous. Young covered with stiff down.

Wild Turkey

Meleagris gallopavo
Plate 6
Pavonine Birds

FAMILY XXXI
Perdicinæ. Partridges

Bill very short, stout, broader than high at the base, with the upper mandible convex, thin edged, obtuse, the lower with the dorsal line convex, the tip rounded. Head small, oblong; neck of moderate length, or rather short; body very bulky. Feet rather of moderate length, stout; tarsus bare, anteriorly scutellate; hind toe rather small, third long, lateral nearly equal, all acute, anterior webbed at the base. Claws moderate, arched, compressed, obtuse. Plumage full and strong, feathers with the plumule much developed.

California Quail

———————————

Callipepla californica
Plate 413
Partridges

Wings rather short, convex, rounded. Tail generally short and rounded, of more than twelve feathers. Tongue triangular, pointed; oesophagus with a very large crop stomach a very strong muscular gizzard, with the lateral muscles highly developed, the epithelium dense, with two concave grinding surfaces; intestine long, and of moderate width. Trachea without inferior laryngeal muscles. Nest on the ground rudely constructed. Eggs numerous. Young covered with stiff down.

Colinus cristatus, Oreortyx pictus
Plate 423
Partridges

FAMILY XXXII
Tetraoninæ. Grouse

Bill short, stout, with the upper mandible convex, thin edged, without notches, its tip thin-edged, obtuse, the lower mandible with the dorsal line slightly convex, the edges thin, the tip rounded. Head small and oblong, neck of moderate length, body very bulky. Feet short, stout; tarsus partially or entirely feathered; hind toe small, third long, lateral nearly equal, all scutellate, anterior webbed at the base. Claws moderate or long, arched, rather depressed, blunt. Plumage fall and soft; feathers with the plumule much developed. Wings rather short, convex, rounded. Tail various, of more than twelve feathers.

Ptarmigan

———

Lagopus mutus
Plate 368
Grouse

A bare coloured space on each side of the neck usually concealed by the feathers, but in some species capable of being distended so as to protrude. A bare red membrane over the eye, more developed in the males. Tongue triangular, pointed; oesophagus with an enormous crop; stomach a very powerful gizzard, having the lateral muscles extremely developed, the epithelium dense, with two concave grinding surfaces; the intestine long and wide. Nests on the ground, rudely constructed. Eggs numerous, spotted. Young covered with stiff down.

Lagopus lagopus
Plate 191
Grouse

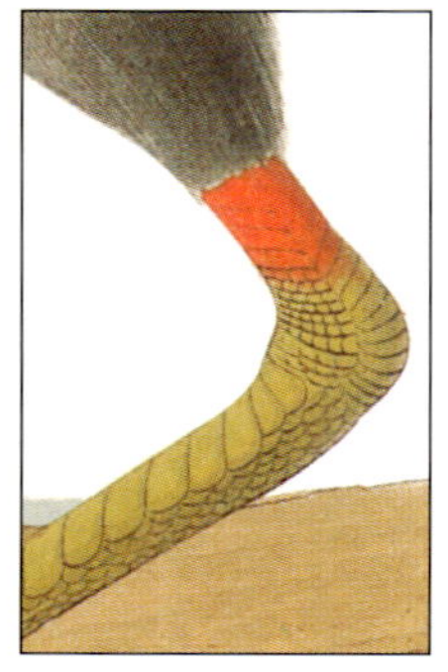

FAMILY XXXIII
Rallinæ. Rails

Bill moderately stout, or slender, short or elongated, compressed, with the point narrow, but obtuse. Head small, oblong, compressed; neck of moderate length, body large, much compressed. Feet large; tibia bare at lower part; tarsus stout, compressed, with very broad, anterior scutella; toes very long, scutellate, marginate; hind toe rather short. Claws long, little arched, compressed, acute. Plumage blended, but stiff. Wings short, convex, rounded, tail very short, rounded.

Common Moorhen

Gallinula chloropus
Plate 244
Rails

Tongue slender, channelled above, tapering to a bristly point; oesophagus long, rather narrow; proventriculus bulbiform; stomach rounded, compressed, very muscular, with the lateral and inferior muscles prominent, the epithelium dense, with two flattish grinding surfaces; intestine long, of moderate width; cloaca globular. Trachea simple, flattened, with a pair of slender inferior laryngeal muscles. Nest bulky, and rudely constructed, on the ground, or supported by grass, or on trees. Eggs numerous, oblong. Young covered with stiff black down.

Fulica americana
Plate 239
Rails

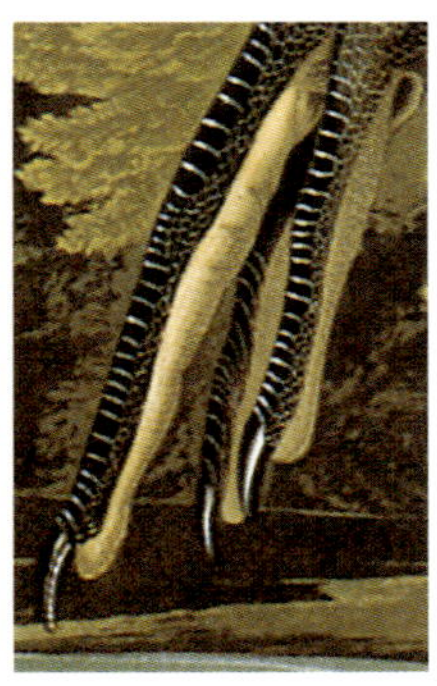

FAMILY XXXIV
Gruinæ. Cranes

Bill about the length of the head, straight, depressed at the base, compressed toward the end, rather obtuse. Nostrils basal, lateral oblong. Head rather small, oblong; neck long; body large, compressed. Legs long and slender; tibia bare at the lower part; tarsus somewhat compressed, anteriorly scutellate; toes rather long, first short and somewhat elevated; claws obtuse. Plumage full and rather compact. Wings broad, convex, the inner secondaries elongated and decurved; tail short, rounded.

Whooping Crane

Grus americana
Plate 226
Cranes

FAMILY XXXV
Charadriinæ. Plovers

Bill short, straight, subcylindrical, obtusely pointed; upper, mandible, with its dorsal line straight for half its length, afterwards convex. Nasal groove bare, extended along two thirds of the length of the bill. Head of moderate size, rather compressed, rounded in front. Eyes large. Neck rather short; body ovate, rather full. Plumage soft, blended, somewhat compact; wings long, pointed, with the first quill longest.

Black-Bellied Plover

Pluvialis squatarola
Plate 334
Plovers

Tail of moderate length, rounded, or with the middle of twelve feathers projecting. Oesophagus of moderate width; stomach rounded, compressed, very muscular, with the epithelium dense and rugous; intestine rather long, and of moderate width. A single pair of inferior laryngeal muscles. Shallow nests on the ground; eggs generally four, large, pyriform, spotted. Young densely covered with down, and able to walk immediately after birth.

Lesser Golden Plover

Pluvialis dominica
Plate 300
Plovers

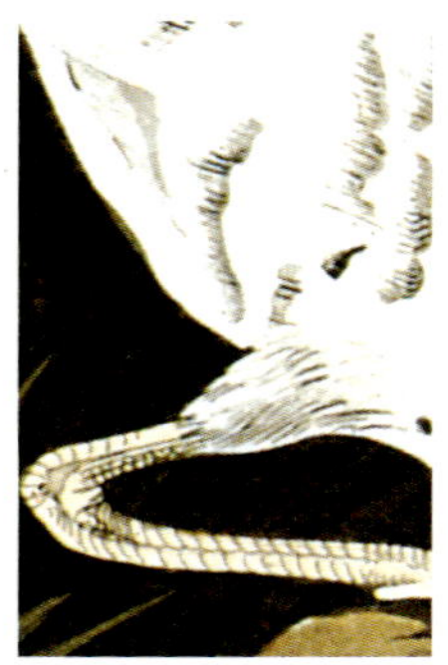

FAMILY XXXVI
Scolopacinæ. Snipes

Bill larger than the head, subulate, slender, straight, recurved, or decurved. Upper mandible with the nasal groove very long, the edges flattened or rounded, the tip generally rather obtuse. Lower mandible with the angle extremely long and narrow, the sides longitudinally grooved. Nostrils basal, linear, small. Head rather small, oblong, anteriorly rounded; neck of moderate length or long; body ovate, deep.

Spotted Sandpiper

Tringa macularia
Plate 310
Snipes

Legs generally long, slender; tarsus long, compressed, scutellate; toes generally four, first small, sometimes wanting; anterior toes of moderate length, slender. Claws small, arched, compressed, rather acute. Wings long, pointed, with the first quill longest, and the inner secondaries tapering and much elongated; tail rather short, of twelve feathers. Tongue long, slender, trigonal, pointed; oesophagus of moderate width, stomach oblong or round, moderately muscular, with dense rugous epithelium; intestine long, of moderate width. Trachea flattened, with a single pair of inferior laryngeal muscles.

White Rumped Sandpiper

Calidris fuscicollis
Plate 278
Snipes

FAMILY XXXVII
Tantalinæ. Ibises

Bill very long, acute, rather stout at the base, obtuse. Nostrils basal, linear or oblong. Head bare in front, rather large or of moderate size; neck long and slender; body ovate. Legs long and rather stout; tibia largely bare; tarsus reticulate, sometimes scaly in front; toes four, articulated at the same level, the anterior webbed at the base, the first more slender.

Glossy Ibis

Plegadis falcinellus
Plate 387
Ibises

Claws arched, compressed, rather obtuse. Wings long and very broad, with the second quill longest. Tail short, of twelve feathers. Tongue triangular, extremely short, flat, and thin. Oesophagus wide; stomach large, muscular, broadly elliptical, with the epithelium dense, longitudinally rugous; intestines generally of moderate length and width, cloaca globular. Trachea without inferior laryngeal muscles.

Scarlet Ibis

Eudocimus ruber
Plate 397
Ibises

FAMILY XXXVIII
Ardeinæ. Herons

Bill longer than the head, stout, tapering, compressed, pointed, its edges often irregularly serrate. Head oblong, compressed; neck very long; body much compressed. Eyes large or moderate. Nostrils basal, linear, longitudinal. Legs long, rather slender; tibia bare to a great extent; tarsus compressed, anteriorly scutellate; toes rather long, the first on the same place, of moderate size, the outer toe a little longer than the inner, and with a slight web at the base; all compressed and scutellate.

Snowy Egret

Egretta thula
Plate 242
Herons

Claws rather long, arched, compressed, acute, that of the hind toe larger and more curved. Plumage blended. Wings long, very broad, with the outer four quills longest, secondaries very long. Tail very short, nearly even, of twelve rather weak feathers. Oesophagus very wide, without dilatation; stomach small, very thin, with the inner coat soft and smooth; intestine very long and extremely narrow; no coecal appendages,

Tricolored Heron

Egretta tricolor
Plate 217
Herons

but the large intestine forming a small sac at its commencement; cloaca very large, globular. Trachea simple, generally cylindrical, with the bronchi wide, and a single pair of slender inferior laryngeal muscles. Nests large, flat, widely constructed, placed on trees, bushes, sometimes on, the ground; eggs from three to four, oval, light blue. Young remain in the nest until fledged.

Great Blue Heron

Ardea herodias
Plate 281
Herons

FAMILY XXXIX
Anatinæ. Ducks

Bill of moderate length, stout, straight, depressed toward the end, obtuse, covered with soft skin; upper mandible transversely convex, with the margins internally lamellate, the tip furnished with a decurved horny broad unguis; lower mandible with the angle long and narrow, the crura slender, flattened, the edges internally lamellate, the tip a flattened unguis. Nostrils elliptical, open, subbasal.

Trumpeter Swan

Cygnus buccinator
Plate 406
Ducks

Head of moderate size; neck long or of moderate length, slender; body full; legs generally short, stout, with little of the tibia bare; tarsus scutellate; toes four, first small; anterior three palmate. Claws moderate, arched, compressed, obtuse. Plumage very full, dense, soft. Wings of moderate length, curved, acute, outer two quills longest. Tail short, of twelve or more feathers. Tongue fleshy, with a median groove, lateral reversed papilla, laminae, or bristles, and a semicircular thin horny tip.

Oesophagus narrow, slightly enlarged at the lower part of the neck; stomach a transversely elliptical gizzard, of which the lateral muscles are excessively developed, the epithelium dense, with two concave grinding surfaces; intestine long and wide; coeca long, cylindrical, contracted at the base. Trachea various, generally much enlarged at the bifurcation, without inferior laryngeal muscles, or only with the slips of the lateral muscles prolonged. Nests generally on the ground, eggs numerous. Young adorned with stiff down, and able to walk and swim from birth.

Canada Goose

Branta canadensis
Plate 277
Ducks

FAMILY XL
Merginæ. Mergansers

Bill rather large, straight, and slender but strong, tapering, higher than broad at the base, nearly cylindrical toward the end. Upper mandible with the dorsal outline sloping gently to the middle, then straight, along the unguis suddenly decurved. The ridge broad and flattened at the base, then convex, the sides sloping, toward the end convex, the edges serrate internally with oblique dentiform lamellae, the unguis oblong, much curved, abruptly rounded at the end.

Red-breasted Merganser

Mergus serrator
Plate 401
Mergansers

The nasal groove is elongated, covered by the soft skin of the bill; lower mandible with the angle very narrow and extended to the unguis, which is obovate, the sides nearly erect, with a long narrow groove, the edges internally serrate, the unguis convex, thick edged. Head rather large and compressed, oblong. Neck of moderate length, body full, depressed, and rather elongated.

Smew

Mergellus albellus
Plate 347
Mergansers

Feet placed far behind, stout; tibia bare for a short space; tarsus very short, compressed, anteriorly covered with small scutella, and another series on the lower half externally. Hind toe very small, with an inferior free membrane; anterior toes half as long again as the tarsus, second shorter than the fourth, which is almost as long as the third, all scutellate, and connected by anteriorly concave webs.

Hooded Merganser

Lophodytes cucullatus
Plate 232
Mergansers

Claws rather small, moderately arched, compressed, acute. Plumage moderately full, dense, soft, glossy, blended beneath. Wings of moderate breadth, convex, acute; inner secondaries elongated and tapering. Tail short, much rounded, of more than twelve feathers. Upper mandible with an internal series of small papillae or laminae on each side, besides those on the margin.

Tongue long, fleshy, emarginated at the base, tapering with a double row of slender reversed papillate along the upper surface,

Common Merganser

Mergus merganser
Plate 331
Mergansers

and two lateral series of filaments on each side, the diameter uniform; stomach a strong gizzard of moderate or small size, with the lateral muscles thick; the epithelium dense and longitudinally rugous; intestine long, rather narrow coeca rather long. Trachea with one or two extensive dilatations, besides the enormously developed tympanum at the bifurcation; no inferior laryngeal muscles. Nests on the ground, or in hollow trees. Eggs numerous.

Brandt's Cormorant

Phalacrocorax penicillatus
Plate 412
Pelicans

FAMILY XLI
Pelecaninæ. Pelicans

Bill longer than the head, rather slender, straight, upper mandible with the ridge separated from the side by a groove, and terminated by a narrow, generally decurved, pointed unguis; lower mandible with the crura elastic and extensile, the angle very long and narrow. Nostrils basal, lateral, linear, small, or obsolete. Space around and before the eye generally bare, as is a portion of the gular sac. Head generally of moderate size, but various; neck long; body elongated, rather slender.

Anhinga

———

Anhinga anhinga
Plate 316
Pelicans

Feet short and stout; tibia bare at its lower part ; tarsus short, very stout, compressed, scaly or scutellate in front; toes four, all connected by webs, and scutellate; first small, fourth longest. Claws short, strong, curved, rather blunt, that of the third toe generally pectinate. Plumage soft, blended, on the back compact and imbricated. Wings long; tail of moderate length, narrow, rounded or tapering.

American White Pelican

Pelecanus erythrorhynchos
Plate 311
Pelicans

Tongue extremely small, triangular, fleshy; oesophagus excessively wide ; a gular sac, sometimes of enormous capacity; proventricular belt generally discontinuous; stomach very small, slightly muscular, epithelium a smooth pyloric lobe; intestine very large and slender; coeca small, cylindrical; cloaca globular. Trachea simple, flattened; no inferior laryngeal muscles.

Double Crested Cormorant

Phalacrocorax auritus
Plate 252
Pelicans

FAMILY XLII
Larinæ. Gulls

Bill of moderate length, straight, compressed, acute upper mandible with the dorsal line generally straight until toward the end, when it is decurved, the ridge convex. The nasal groove is rather long, the edges sharp, direct, overlapping, the tip rather acute and declinate; lower mandible with the angle long and very narrow, the dorsal line ascending and nearly straight, with an angular prominence at its commencement.

Bonaparte's Gull

Larus philadelphia
Plate 324
Gulls

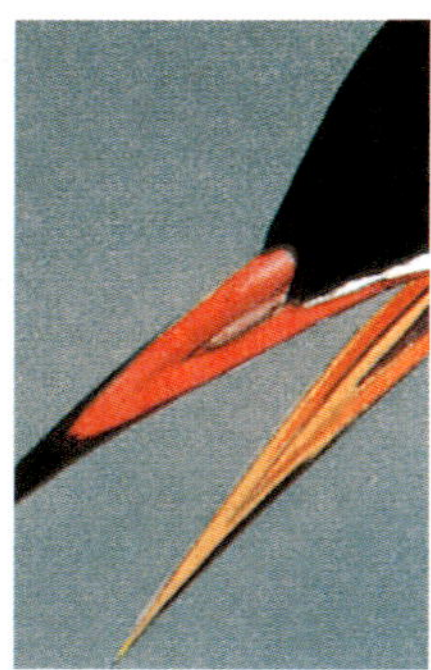

Nostrils submedial or basal, oblong. Head of moderate size, ovate; neck of moderate length ; body rather stout. Legs short or of moderate length; tibia bare at its lower part; tarsus anteriorly scutellate; toes four, the first very small, free, the third longest; anterior toes connected by webs. Claws small, arched, compressed, rather acute. Plumage full, soft, blended, and somewhat compact on the back and wings, the latter long and pointed; tail of twelve feathers, even, rounded, or emarginate.

Common Tern

Sterna hirundo
Plate 309
Gulls

Tongue long, slender, pointed; oesophagus very wide; stomach rather small, moderately muscular, with a dense, longitudinally rugous-epithelium; intestine of length and width. Trachea simple, with a single pair of inferior laryngeal muscles. Nests on the ground, rudely constructed. Eggs few, not exceeding four, spotted. Young covered with down.

Sterna forsteri, Sterna trudeaui
Plate 409
Gulls

FAMILY XLIII
Procellarinæ. Fulmars

Bill generally shorter than the head, moderately stout, compressed. Upper mandible with the ridge formed of two generally united plates, at the anterior part of which, usually about half the length of the bill, are the nostrils; the sides separated by a groove, the tip a decurved, compressed, pointed unguis. Lower mandible with the angle very long and narrow, the tip more or less decurved.

Northern Fulmar

Fulmarus glacialis
Plate 264
Fulmars

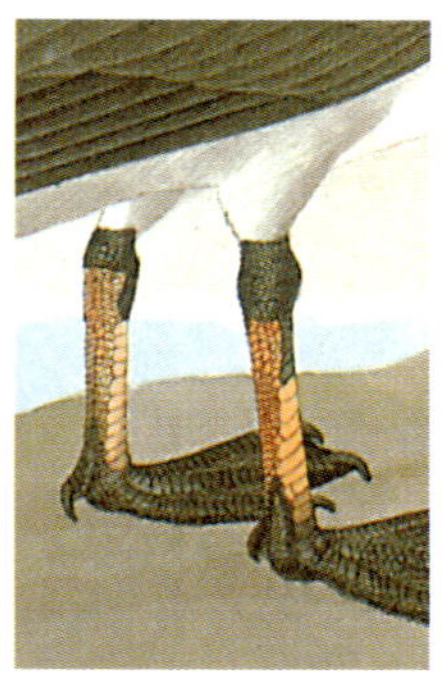

Head of moderate size, ovate, neck of moderate length; body compact. Feet of ordinary length, rather slender; tibia bare below for a short space; tarsus little compressed, anteriorly scutellate; toes four, the first extremely small and elevated, with a conical deflected claw; anterior toes webbed; the third and fourth nearly equal. Claws arched, compressed, acute.

Stercorarius longicaudus
Plate 267
Fulmars

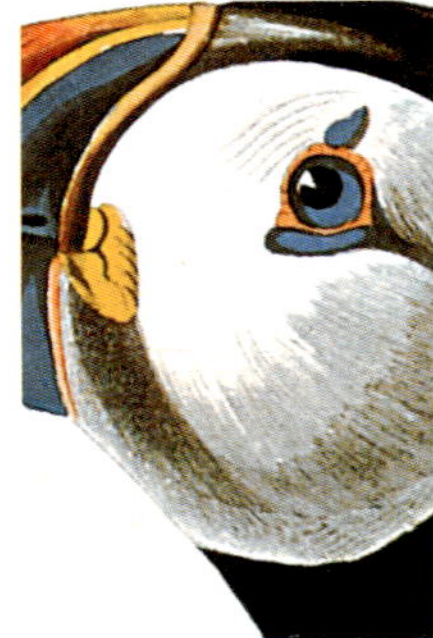

Plumage full, soft, rather compact. Wings long, rather broad and pointed, the first quill generally longest. Tail short, of from twelve to sixteen feathers. Oesophagus very wide, often enormously dilated, especially at its lower part, stomach small and moderately muscular; intestine of moderate length. Trachea simple, with a single pair of inferior laryngeal muscles.

Fratercula artica
Plate 213
Auks

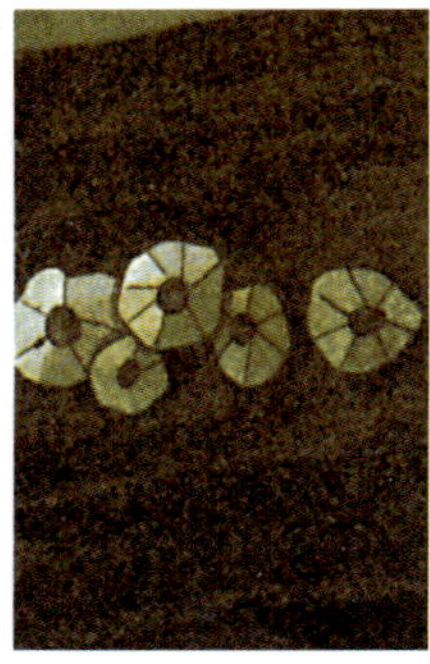

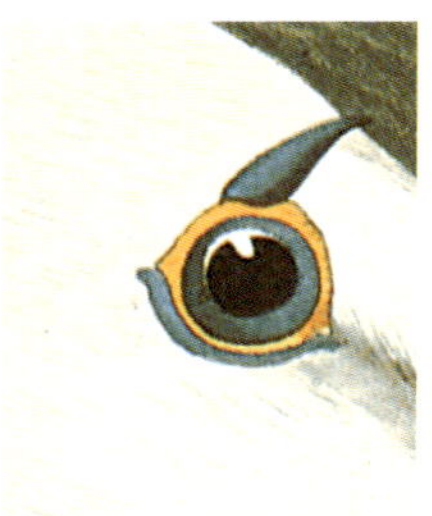

FAMILY XLIV
Alcinæ. Auks

Bill shorter than the head, much compressed, generally very high, in the species approaching the next family rather slender. Nostrils small, linear, basal, and submarginal. Head large, broadly ovate, anteriorly narrowed; neck short and thick; body full, compact, ovate, or somewhat elongated. Feet short, rather stout, placed far behind; tibia bare for a short space; tarsus very short, compressed, anteriorly scutellate;

Horned Puffin

Fratercula corniculata
Plate 293
Auks

toes three, of moderate length, scutellate, webbed. Claws strong, arched, acute. Plumage dense, blended, soft. Wings small, narrow, pointed. Tail very short. Tongue slender, trigonal; oesophagus very wide, within the thorax extremely dilated ; stomach rather large, muscular, with the epithelium dense and longitudinally rugous; intestine long and wide. Trachea simple, with a single pair of inferior laryngeal muscles. Egg generally single.

Black Guillemot

Cepphus grylle
Plate 219
Auks

FAMILY XLV
Columbinæ. Divers and Grebes

Bill the length of the head, straight, rather stout, much compressed, pointed; upper mandible with the dorsal line declinate, almost straight, or towards the end convex; nasal groove rather long, feathered at the base. Nostrils basal, linear, direct, pervious. Feet stout, short, placed extremely far behind; tarsus extremely compressed; toes four, the first very small, and lobed.

Common Loon

Gavia immer
Plate 306
Divers and Grebes

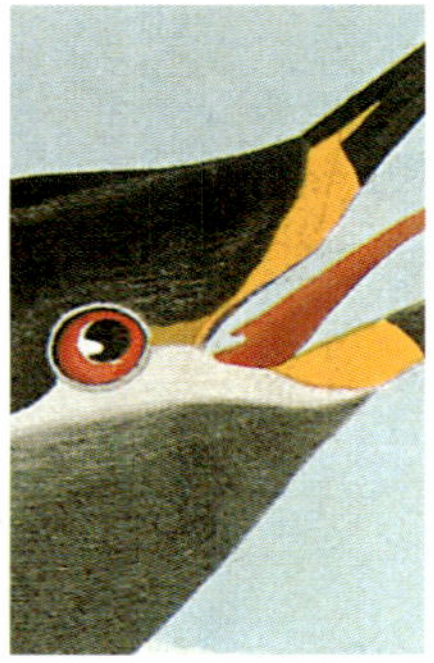

The anterior united by webs, which in some are lobed. Plumage dense, short, glossy, and generally silky beneath. Wings small, very narrow, acute. Tail very short, sometimes extremely small, and forming a slight tuft. Tongue slender, trigonal, tapering; oesophagus very wide in its whole length, or narrowed in the anterior part with the proventriculus wide; stomach generally large, muscular, with a dense rugous epithelium; intestine rather long and wide.

Red-necked Grebe

Podiceps grisegena
Plate 298
Divers and Grebes

Index